EXCAVATIONS

SERA MADDOX DRAKE

Contents

Foreword: About These Poems

These poems are old.

I originally wasn't going to publish them commercially, but the little collection of poems that I published on Wattpad as a way to put them in cloud storage got over two thousand views.

Then it won an Amby award, which is one of the most prestigious awards any collection of poetry can win on Wattpad.

Then one of my readers asked me to publish it commercially so she could *buy* it.

And I thought, well. Gosh. Maybe my poetry is worth more than just storing on a cloud.

So here they are. These are not all of the poems I've written; they're just some of my better poems.

An astute reader might notice that the voice I use is nearly always feminine. It's been quite a while since I've written poetry – I write more often in prose now. That might not be coincidental. I am transgender. I have been using the singular *they* to describe myself for the past ten years, to reflect the fact that I don't feel like I am a woman anymore. I wasn't that great at being a woman to begin with, but when I wrote poetry, I generally wrote it when I was in "girl mode," so to speak, and my default for many years has been neutral. I am genderfluid, but although I experience occasional disconcerting bursts of femininity or masculinity, most of the time I'm simply gender-naked – agender. It's changed me in a number of ways, and I suspect one of the things that changed was my literary voice. I write more in prose now. (Some of you might already have read *Ancilla* and/or *Morsels: Tales of Love and Passion* already, in which case, you're familiar with my prose).

This collection of poetry was an exercise in archaeology, hence the title of the anthology.

I hope you enjoy browsing the artifacts.

UNDERNEATH

JUVENILIA: 1989 - 1991

The Gift of Prometheus

It burns in me still:
the silken bridal veil cast over the twilight
only barely shielding the smoldering sunset;
the music of Rimsky-Korsakov,
driving like a lance into my heart,
gentle painful forcing of beauty;
the moonlight that lies on the grass,
sipping the furtive dew.
It burns in me.
The candle in my soul begins to sear through.
Fire, pure and painful,
caressing me, rending my flesh,
begging yet demanding to be released.
The world is aflame.
And I stare in joyful agony at the candelabra,
unable to partake of the supper set before me,
feasting rather on the tender danger of the flames -
at the painful beauty of a dark room
set by jewels of candle-fire,
shadow fighting against the unquenchable burning.
The candlelight burns itself into my eyes,
showing me the elegant dance
of tragedy and myth -
I am consumed by fire.

The fire will not let me go!

And in this mating of heaven and hell,

pleasure and torment, innocence and loss,

burning and shadow,

I am entranced, made helpless in my deadly moth's fascination

with the flame that beckons to me,

demanding a lover's firey union.

It burns in me still.

A Passion

I kneel, in false penance,
on these sharp stones of anguish
until my bare knees bleed
pain on pain;
and I wait for a sign
of your presence
until I have long since not heard
the voice of my defeat;
and it is only when I cry out
to protest your absence
that I realize that it is I
who am not with you.

It occurs to me, oh long-suffering lover,
that I address you
in the same way
that I might address my God.
I wonder who listens
to my wolflike howl.

Supper

It is myself and I again
in this dark room
while I sit across the long table
from my alter ego
And she asks me to pass the rolls
so I pass them
and then pour the wine.
And we sit, silent,
and she bores herself into my eyes
while I busy myself with the peas.
I look away
and she looks away
and we both long for some dinner music
to break the silence
of our hostility.

My Lady

Pools of night mist in her eyes
my princess of dusk gazes
into her wine-glass
as the firelight runs across her cheek.
Swaying shoulders and dancing laugh,
the joy and trembling shake her
like a blossom in a spring gust
as she twirls to the piper's music.
Dreams and passions
reserved for pure knights in armor:
my high one is sought
by mad poets and gentle lunatics -
and as the world rotates
around her magic castle
the sun sets, the piper rests, her lunatic runs
to chase the moon.

Dream and Reality

I dream of his face
and of falling into twin pools of mystery
as he looks toward me
with that knowing smile,
as the light shines -

He is gazing at the fountain in the square.

I sit and float into the stratosphere
as he stands in front of the bench
that I sit on, and I smile
as he turns toward me,
I try to act blank
while he teases me for inattentiveness -

He is talking to a girl that I don't even know.

I ponder and puzzle
over this mysterious almost-stranger of a man,
and try to think of pleasant safe thoughts
like monogamy, and noodles
that are eaten late at night with greedy fingers
while my heart plays spin the bottle
and I gasp as he looks at me

and tears off my clothes with his eyes -

He is staring into space, thinking of medieval castles.

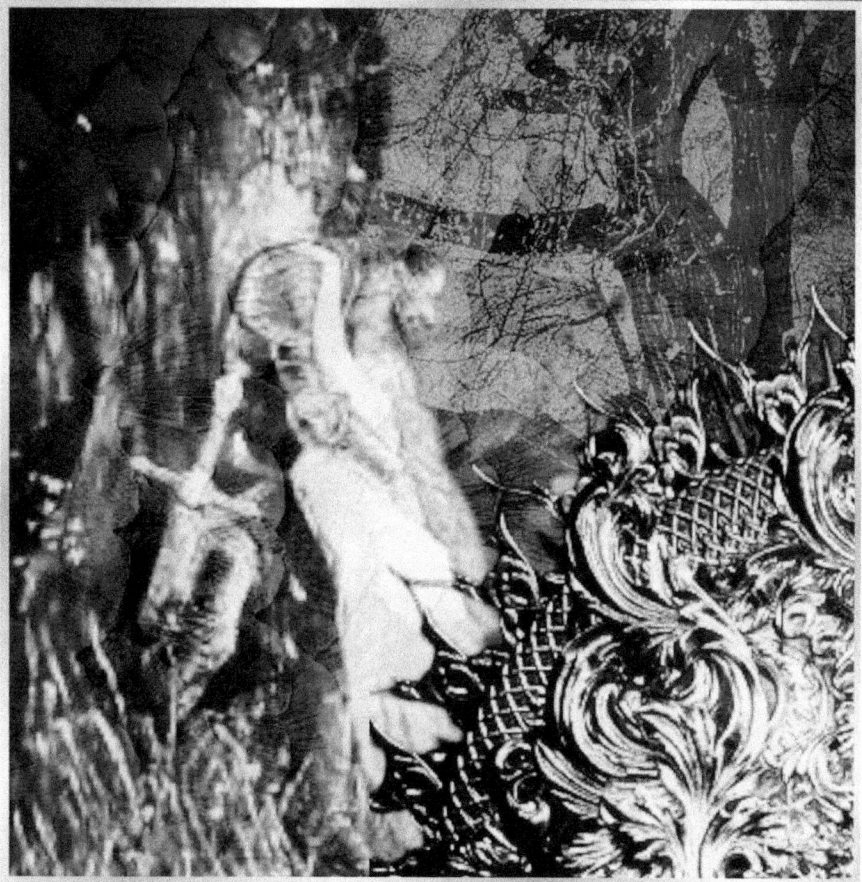

Longing

This strange and beautiful anguish;
This passion that sweeps fire across my breast -
It chokes within me -
I cannot speak
My limbs, weak like newborns,
tremble to rise
from the floorboards.
I cry aloud in tongues not of my making,
I shake with every effort
to vacate my body,
to fly like a zephyr to your side
Oh, love, feel for my absence.
Reach for my empty air.

An Evening Promenade

It is peaceful and quiet
and the summer night is only a summer night,
I am alone with my thoughts
and my self
and I breathe the air
free from the disturbing touch
of hostile mankind.

Sounds of beer and laughter
appear before me
and nod their greetings.
They have just stepped out of the neighbor's door
to escape the party for a little fresh air.
I respond politely and pass on.

I am, once again, alone...for God's sake, my love,
why are you not with me?

Epithalamion: In Honor of a Most Worthy Opponent

No more strains of decision, no more the dance,
The sparring is over. You sprawl on my arms and legs,
exhausted from our wrestling, content with your victorious loss -
and I spit a strand of your hair from my mouth,
and grin at nothing, or perhaps at something.
And that is all. No more time to debate
the why's and wherefore's and but-what-if's
now that the time has gone: no time, but truce.
We lay in peace, a lion and a unicorn,
spirit and strength, at rest, like slain heroes
or star-crossed lovers.

Courting the Muse

I set my pen to paper
and say the prayer to summon my other self
and she appears, smiling like a muse
who has just taken half a hit of acid
and probably some poor virgin's innocence, as well –

Politely, for once, I ask in meek and deferential tones
if she has seen my better nature anywhere recently;
it seems to be gone, along with my guilt
and my familial ties and my money;
for I had always assumed that the other three
brought the first along
like a distant and priggish maiden aunt –

And the muse laughs,
and tells me how much nicer I am
now that I'm not trying to protest my innocence,
tells me she's glad to enjoy getting laid for a change
and as a parting shot before she returns
to her couch on the Olympian heights,
informs me that my poetry
is still as rotten as ever

and I thank her gravely
and cease to torment my notebook.

Mysteries

O Brave New World

for Mary Shelley

"Satan's despair is absolute because Satan, as pure spirit, is pure consciousness, and for Satan (and all men in his predicament) every increase in consciousness is an increase in despair." - Soren Kierkegaard

THE MONSTER SPEAKS:

Born in this new land
again, from weary parts already resurrected,
I stare and stare at the sea
because I have never seen before
that which is ocean. What is ocean?
but a great pregnant goddess,
heaving to give birth, yet ready
to swallow up any, all,
to feed the hungry void that is the foetus
that was her heart. Swallow me not,
for I have yet to experience the joys
of walking on water. Earth lighter than air,
and water conquered by a fire
that is I...I shall swallow that water up,
and out of my music of profoundest despair

shall sing my song of fire,

of being surrounded by all-burning flame. I,

bringer of fire, creation of fire,

destruction of fire - Quench this fire!

oh you merciless creator, you who gave birth

to your monstrous creation.

It burns too bright, this pure black flame,

this misery of existing knowing.

To know is a prison. To be is a torment -

being in this existing knowing -

and the universe gives no assent

but a command; and the command is

know.

Heloise

In the chapel, falling to one's knees,
one is prone to visions:
visions of angels, of the empyreal layers
of heaven, of the face of one's God:
and the face of love.
A single tail-feather from the Holy Dove
is my relic, that I pray before.
Praying for visions. O Venus
have mercy on me!

    for it is his face I see
at matins, at compline,
at every calling to prayer -
and at vespers, especially at vespers,
dusk is the cruelest time of all -
this vision of eternal love;

    unreachable, untouchable,
beautiful beyond compare
is the face of my lord -

    My God -

Teacher, friend, husband.
It seems only yesterday
that we last made love:
in the secret of the chapel,
the holy chants of the sisters
echoing from the cloister,
only our father witnessing
the consummation.
Holy Sacrament it was. The body of my lord,
the outpouring of my lord,
shed for love's sake
in secret marriage, sacred secret bonds
of holy wedlock.

My God. I had his son.
Astrolabe. The device used
to measure Heaven's distance.

And now he is gone. I, poor sinner,
can only see his face
in tormented visions -
would that he could be resurrected!
I long for the life after death that is to come,
eternal love, eternal life,
whether it be in the heaven
of his sweet speech,
or the fires of his passion...
it will all be the same.
For what is Hell,
but to be separated from one's Lord?
Am I not in hell suffering now?

Surely when I am called
all my sins will be purged,
forgiven; forgotten.

  Sic et non he asked me. And I responded,
Yes. Yes, I will follow you.
Through the gates. I will follow you forever.
Even into Hell.

  And now, manless, wed to one
who unmanned himself when his manhood was lost,
I have only the face of the Divine
to console me. Bride of Christ!
Where is my faithless lover?

  Even his name, I mouth in prayer -
  Abelard. A strange prayer
in this chapel, where all prayers
are mumbled in Latin
for an unknown God;
but I, who am chaste as Mary,
have had visions of my saviour,
one who will come when my existence is finished
and will carry me, at last, to safety.
  Abelard, I pray. *O come
and have mercy on me.*

The Chapel of Love

"I went to the Garden of Love... And I saw that it was filled with graves... And Priests in black gowns were making their rounds, And binding with briars my joys and desires." - William Blake

I made a journey by ferry
to the Chapel of Love; and entered,
naked, hair flowing like Godiva,
holding a bouquet of lilies
in my hand of making and destroying;
garlands of thorned roses were my only shields.
I did not go on hands and knees,
though custom and past passion plays demanded it;
I walked, brazen and curious,
braving the sharp stained glass
with my eyes. And I was pierced for it.
The knight with his lance rode me
and claimed me as his palfrey;
his squires anointed my flesh
with streaks of stained glass
until I was no more than a figure of glass
in a medieval window.
Such is the penance for pride

when one stands before the altar of sacrificing.
Yet I walked on, eyes daring, feet striding,
flowers dangling like broken manacles,
until I stood before my lord and master
and proclaimed with one sharp vorcel cry
my single vowel. "I am I," I cried,
crying "I" - until with a shriek,
the walls fell down in so much stone
and shattered glass.

Edda

I. The Voyage

Here at the northern beginning
of the world serpent,
the waters are clear cold silver,
the sun glints gold
on silver. Here the waves under your ship
are the rough-heaving shoulders of warriors;
gold on silver engraved in armour.
A conquest, cattle and gold and women
and bronze torques, to bring home to the wife
who waits for you, here;
hoe in hand, hair gleaming gold
against silver.

II. Yggdrasil (the serpent under the waters)

The waves throwing themselves at the shore
raking the shore with long wailing fingernails
that stream in moon-darkness.
And in the maiden moon
the shore consents,
gives in, the shore gives up its sands

to the night-vaulted sea.

These are the shores of night;
on this dream sea,
no means yes, hold is a cry of terror,
the mouth mouths
a prayer against twilight.

III. Odin's Hall

I have wandered Midgard
hero-like for so many years now,
so long that the leaves' frost
fallen no longer speaks of light's end,
merely of winter, of the gathering-in
before storms. The cry of ravens
in a weird tongue,
flight of thought and memory
against empty sky -
faugh! how this mead is sour
on my tongue! I long for the well
of my home, the clear-honey
wine, the warmth of my hearth,
the welcome of my own beloved
in my own bed. I have been here
too long. When will the horns call for me,
rainbow-trumpeting?

Interview With a Muse

for Anne Rice (presented to her in person at a book signing)

Night time: solitude: fallen curtains
The parents have gone to their separate beds
and I to mine.
In this my solitary tower
I keep my vigil -

I light a votive
against night's darkness
and carry it to my closet. There,
amid the shoes and sneakers and Sunday dresses,
I say my novena. The uniform skirts,
garish in blue and green and black tartan riot,
have become stained glass windows.
I no longer notice
that I kneel on saddle shoes -

Darkness has fallen.
Little has changed since puberty.
In the closet, shut tight against the world
I kneel on piles of black leather articles,

mouthing prayers to a goddess
whose name I barely know

(chrome hooks clacking like rosary beads)

the books of recitations, well-thumbed like missals,
become sweat-stained, dog-eared,
used.

Lady, your prayers for me
are well spent -

I have been at vespers
and faithfully I light candles
where the darkness touches my corners;
I take communion
of red wine and printed parchment.
There, where my hands have been touched by page
is a mark of the holy,
a stigmata of quill.

But how can one be saved
who asks for no mercy,
no deliverance from sin?

Every night,
by the candle,
by the book,
I am delivered
unto darkness

and my soul sears
like fire.

Special Interests

For my next hobby,
I believe I will take up birdwatching.
Not that I dislike sex, mind you –
the play is fun, the politics engrossing
and the people who seduce me,
downright fascinating. It's just that
I want to see the faces of all my friends
when I inform them of this new pursuit:
"What?" they will ask, stunned.
"It's so noncontroversial, so safe.
Can't you at least take up bungee jumping?"
Ah, me. You see, once you're an established pervert
your pursuits are always suspect.
They'll never take your model airplanes seriously
unless the blueprints can be proved
to have sadomasochistic overtones,
or (at the very least) you've painted
a pink triangle or a riding crop on the left strut.
But birdwatching it will be.
I shall even endeavor not to sermonize
about the strange proclivities
of the yellow-bellied sapsucker,
or to court my would-be lovers

with my latest kinky impersonation
of the Baltimore oriole.

Drink Deeply From Summer's Cup

Drink deeply from summer's cup
and drown laughing in yellow dandelions –
This is the first and greatest commandment.
Suffer gladly through your step-stone lessons,
through the falling backs and the letting goes,
creep cheerfully in the cold almost-dawns
for your taste of sun-drunkenness.
For in the frost that follows
is the metallic taste of cold.
Hands grow lines where palms grow short,
silver crowns regal heads where once was gold,
and in every musky corner hovers the shadow lover,
smiling coyly; asking you, Is it not time
to come to my perfumed bed?
This is the note you hear. Drink.
Only in such inebriation is the light so sweet,
the grass so fragrant.

Observations Of The Eclipse, 10 May 1994, At Midday

for D.H.Lawrence
"O build your ship of death,
for you will need it..."

The park shimmers
in a grey-silver almostlight,
a foreshadowing
of moon.
It is not enough

and so I go in deeper,
winding along paths
of half-clad trees

tracing the waters.

There is foretold a conjunction
of Mercury, Venus,
Hades, moon, planets once joined
with Neptune
at my birth

Where darkening was a sky
already twilight colored

I am going into the forest
to see
the silvering of the sun

*

Across the picnic meadow
where before me is forest
and beside me
walk
a grey goose, a white dog

the water is shining

I chart ripples, mirrors
I fashion a ship
of bark.

*

My journey
slides
deeper into
the trees

A goose cries,
flaps its wings,

diving against water
for food.

What is the time
is it time?

There is no time here,
but the time is coming -
indeed there will be time -
Time to go in deeper
into the shadow and silver
light

It is the time

It is getting brighter
I am going into the light
here
on my knees
sand crawling up flesh

It is the time

and so I make my journey
into the sun
braving the end
for a glimpse

as my eyes cringe
look up
and gaze

into

silver

*

Only a moment. One scant moment.
Was that it? I did not see
anything, really.
A blinding brightness.
A little crescent
of sun and moon
reflected through leaves.

I shake sand and twig
from my shoes
and squint against a world
burned into retina:
a mocking ring of silver,
a brilliant stream;

And alive,
in the trees,
in the lapis of sky -
I am alive as sun
as I smash a mosquito

between thumb and forefinger.

A silvery juice
is all that remains.

The Bind of Flow

It is the darkest blindfold
that covers the eyes of my sight.
Only in the darkest night
do I guide my steps inch by inch,
tracing the cold wet paths
of an underground stream.

Spiraling towards the navel-center
(my sex bound in umbilicus)
touched by unseen hands, I am swept away
on tides of night
in a cradle of ecstasy

I am a silent goddess

Lost in this I cry out
to drown on gasping my first cold air,
to not recognize the strong hands
that have pulled me forth here
and baptized me in pomegranate tattoos

Storm Sky

The clouds are pregnant with grey storms and I,
sitting on the cushioned couch in a public lounge,
surrounded in amniotic purple, labour with my pen
as I contemplate the snow. Cracked hands,
hands of winter, grip this pen. I seep as I melt.
Oozed out in blood, my words seep slowly,
onto drifts of white paper. What soil will I flood
when springtime comes to dance? What flowers
will feed from this dying pool? What poems will scream
as they gasp their first cold air?

Autumn

Lead me down passages
of amniotic darkness
where autumn's heart beats like thunder,
where the world pushes against me
drawing me into layers of earth
and fallen leaves.

Does the night speak
in whispering tongues? Listen
to the wind in the naked branches
of trees, the soft pattering of sleet
at the window. It speaks of falling.

Fragments

There is violence in the wind tonight
I can feel it deep within,
it wants to carry me away -
wet leaves scatter adrift
on the night air, and the streetlamp is a bemused sentry

*

   I stand in the rain,
the laughing wind sinking claws
into my chill, shadows pattering into the street,
oozing into the gutter. The moonless night
shines in artificial halo,
my wan moon face caught in a beam
cries tears. Winds, have mercy,
do not lash me
with your gasps of sharp desire

Diet of Worms

By doctor's orders, as of 10 May 1994,
I am to go onto a homeopathic diet
of no carbohydrates and no saturated fats
and no hybrids - so I suppose it is time
to put up my trailing rags, to dress sensibly
and read Jane Austen. I can see the sense of it.
This romantic starving poet diet is killing me.

    I can give up the macaroni and cheese
(if I never look at another box again
I couldn't be happier), the oodles of Romulan noodles,
the Byron, the Goethe - the sorrows
of young Sarah - but no sugars?
What about the sweet Napoleons, the eclairs,
puffs of pastry Ionesco melting in my mouth?
No more sweetly-dripping baklava or Sapphic honey cloying
to end my repasts? No Ossian?
Not even a bit of Bernard da Ventadorn, when the days
are long in May? ah God, ah God, the dawn
how soon it comes!

    My mouth waters for lasagna, cannoli,
and for the sweet liebestod endness of concupiscent curds
(no ice cream, I can't have that anymore, dairy is death)
for scallops and Swinburne and shrimp
in a milky white sauce, for the divine Marquis I can never afford

oh please, at least let me keep my dogeared *Story of O*
tooth-rotting Turkish delight!

Grease or Death

Today is a perfect day for a little hookey,
I say as I seek my death from cancer,
and so it goes that I do the dirty deed;
it is time to impersonate the sun worshipper.
But of course there are complications -
Halfway into the burning ritual, I run into
a god. There must be leash laws somewhere about that,
about letting your gods go loose.
Things are just not the way they were...
We greet. We make silence. I remember
that my flesh is slowly rotting in the ultraviolet,
and this sparks a brief flash of intelligence -
enough for me to babblingly pronounce,
I was not made for the sun. It's a redhead thing,
we're all closet vampires. It is probably
not tacit agreement when the stray god informs me
that with sunscreen I now have a choice
between grease and death. Though in his innocence
he has spoken truth (I am screened, and sticky.)
Grease or death rings through my mind.
Why do the gods always make *you* responsible
for choosing? Now he invites me to darkness,
under the student dormitories. I smile in silence.
Somewhere, I must have accepted a choice.

Words

Spoiled meat; spoiled rotten; spoiled brat; spare
the rod and you spoil the child;
spoiled earth; spoilers on cars
that go very fast, racing like the wind -
not heeding red lights. Scarlet pimpernel; scarlet
letters; Scarlett O'Hara, who will always have Tara;
diminutive scar that can't be seen;
woman with red hair, who is born a witch;
Harvard crimson; scarlet gown: the lady in red. She walks
in the night, like beauty, and all that's best
of dark and bright meet in her aspect. Damaged
goods; broken goods; soiled goods; soiled hands,
loam-coloured hands: a gardener's hands, digging
deep in the earth, rooting up tares,
sowing seeds that will become
lovely lilies, unless they become cherry blossoms.
It's a quirk of nature, a property
of soil. Mad Magdalen goes on dirty toes.
Fallen leaves, falling in love, windfallen
fruits, falling down stairs, falling
from an aeroplane; fall as a season;
fall as a verb; fall as a description;
fall as a spiritual state of being. The fall of Eve,
falling down drunk, fallen hopelessly, fallen hard.

Fear of falling. Waterfalls. I've fallen
and can't get up. My skin's bruised, but
I've survived. It comes from having earth
in my chart.

Vegetarianism

I had the strangest urge today:
I was consumed by a desire to eat trees.
I was just sitting there innocently,
in my bed, listening to heavy metal shriekback
and doing an expository comparison of Holmes to Watson,
and then it hit and I had to,
simply *had to* run out into the woods and sink my teeth
into the nearest sycamore.
Sycamore, because a hickey would show up
so sweetly on that mottled flesh.
Never mind that I live in the inner city
where there aren't any trees, and trees don't
get hickeys when you suck them dry
anyway. All I could think about
was that tree groaning in ecstasy;
and me, sating myself mercilessly,
teeth plunging, sticky sweet sap running
in delirious rivulets of white blood cells
from my mouth...And then!
And then I'd thank the tree kindly
and make love to a mulberry bush!
Shake the berries from its streaming loins!
But it's November, my better nature moans -
And I answer with a whoop and a howl

and seek tulips to kiss, and rhododendrons.
Rhododendrons to romp in,
roses to row in. And the crowning glory
is that I shall wallow in mushrooms
until I give birth to a puffball.
I want to get knocked up with fungal secrets,
balloon away on the spores of the wind.
It all begins with misanthropism,
I decide, as I vampirize a salacious carrot.
Vegetarianism is oh so elite.

Roi Polloi

This from one who sees the sun
sailing on celestial roads rich and
red: oh, see! and say, can you see
the sun king's chariot spoked
with smoking lynch-pins burning red
on raw skies? His red hair fire
burning wheels against seas
of lead sky. Stay, do not rue
the road you say you saw
open up to the red chariot sun
to burn raw through sea and sky.
Red horses pulling regally
the fabulous sun, across the sky.

The Ideal Form of Spring

Robins at full blast, singing of mating, singing
the joy of eating fat worms – dandelions –
White violets, bachelor's buttons, tender weeds
of white that sway in sudden winds – white
crab-rose petals, white clouds marching
across blue sky (painfully blue sky).
Sudden warm rains that fickly become ice,
sodden grass: green emerald grass that
bursts under foot, green grassy clover, green
smells – green shoots! Maples! Maples
that multiply! burgeon forth, become a galaxy
of fluttering green wings, green shooting maples!
making merry destruction of green lawns,
and gutters and gardens – young maples,
stubborn maples, all-over maples – and the robins –

Plato, sweet friend, you were wrong. This came first.

Crossing the Waters

It's an anticipation, not unlike
the time you had to get up in front
of the whole third grade and recited
that passage from the Tibetan book.
A shiver. Your stomach contracts
and you taste cold sweat. But then
it's time to be off and so you clutch
your loved one's hands, your stuffed bear, your identification;
and knowing yourself to be alone
you get on board. All strapped in
and engines revving, roaring
to get off - and then you're lifted
dizzyqueasy off the ground,
fear of flying, of a strange land
making sourness in the hollow pressure within
against which you swallow. It's your throat,
it's only your throat...And you're sick now,
really officially sick, but
it's *alea iacta est* from now on
because you can see the clouds under
your flightpath - and the turbulence
from your heart going thudthudthud
against the cabin is your only bolster
against the groundless terror of leaving.

Of flight against the world. It's a sort
of death. Your revolt against your body.
Your head that screams in the arms
of the restraining stewardesses, as you make
your descent into the underworld:
How many seeds did you eat? enough
to wish yourself trapped forever,
even if it's only a season, a scant
year of it. Time to pay your ferryman,
to give in to the customs
of your strange new land. Your cavern
is now your home.

Chain

In the quest for delicious survival
let us not forget the vein:
blue under its gauzes of flesh,
it pumps and pulses and gushes red
sweetly into the mouth. Sweet fruity
and salty with just the right metal
vinegar, how it gushes, as if willingly!
As if the bruised flesh underneath
did not really mind the abuse.

   Abstinence is absurd. From whence does meat come
save the bleating lamb, the sad-eyed stupid
lowing cow? Vegetables die, screaming
as they are ripped from the earth,
the wheat losing its generations
along with life to fill the bowels
of some large and powerless being.
Hunger is the great leveler,
it cuts away all pretense to greatness
of soul. Even the virtuous and good hunger,
and pay court to the banner of rose
and scythe. No arts or works could grow else
so let us thank death.

Even the windfallen fruits and nuts
are dropped egg and sperm: life that almost was,
that was not.

Eat the tender flesh, enjoy the orgy
love-feasting on this offering of artery. You cannot live
without this suffering. You cannot live
without the joy of death.

Communion

It's a terrible thing
to feel the bones crunch
beneath your teeth,
flesh tearing off and getting caught
to linger, accusing,
on the roof of your mouth.
To gnaw, after long years
of abstinence. To chew.
The dust of the road,
already choking in your throat,
mingles with the dust of bones
and fleshy parts
and chokes you.
You eat, and you die as you eat,
and death refuses to hurry.

And then, sweet relief!
the blood pouring down your throat,
merciful release, sweet firey liquid,
terrible and giving,
terrible in its giving.
All is drowned.
All thought of need, all hunger
for sense and meaning,

is held under the river, drowned.
Nothing survives this.
You are left shaking and naked,
a wan spirit, skin and bones
ripped away,
body taut with newness,
aching for this strange comfort.

After this, all food is
too solid, all drink too weak,
and the sun burns harsh,
bringing tears to your eyes.

To P. B. S.

Shelley, I too know what it is
to hear the siren call of death
in cold, deep waters. All too heavily
I have felt the weight of the past
on my shoulders. And I know
at what your biographers only barely hinted:
you went willingly into the cold.
For we two are one, we who are distracted
by the dins of our egos, by
the loud revels of unseen unseelie fairies,
the noisy exuberance of crows just before dawn.

You went willingly, until the end
when you went down; the water slid her thin hand
around your throat, and squeezed;
her grip more powerful than any you could have imagined.
I know that at the last you struggled
and gasped in brine and tried to claw
your way to freedom: too late. One last flare
of lightning, one last gulp of the sea,
and you could not resist.

Hypnotized by the blare of the horn,
five hundred feet from your tomb,

I stood still as marble
and did not notice the rain pelting down
until I was hit by the bus, and down,
swearing for my life. My lungs crushed by terror and pain,
I could not even writhe against the firey water
that threatened to consume me.
I felt the icy fingers of rain caress my mouth
and knew that we were one, you and I. I knew to shake
in the presence of a passing flood.

I who have committed suicide
and lived to tell the tale, trembled in pain
and called out to a god who I had renounced,
and shook for fear of losing my life.

You did not go gently into the good night,
Shiloh my alter self. You kicked and swore and wrestled
against a watery angel, you begged
at the last. Your tomb (with its Lycidas
that does mercy to the scarred maggot
that washed ashore in the wake of your death)
is mute. Still, I knew the truth,
in a second between flash and echo.

Orphic Hymn

Three silver notes, moonlit agony,
falling tears from the lyre. The gravid moon.
The earth stands still, hush of pain,
long silenced in black reaches
of tumulus mound. Still stands the moon,
Orpheus knocking at the gate; and then
great mighty howl! hell awaits him.

   No flowers are scattered this time,
no chariot receives him,
he walks into inner reaches
helixing. His feet are too slow.
And the road is marked with blood:
he is heavy, heavy, lead and gold
where he steps but for his tears,
soft falling rain, he belongs here in this earth,
he is of earth. The spirits pass,
they marvel at his chthonic glow
his gentian torch.

   They hear a cry from beyond,
strange music, from where can it come?
It goads them. He is alone when he reaches

the boat. He has no coin, no soul.
His soul has already been paid -

so the ferryman shakes his head:
the last ferry has already been made,
and besides that, Master Orpheus, you'll sink
the boat with your lead-heavy flesh -

But the song carries them. Song
of hell, from hell, from the depths
of the heart; the lyre smiles,
drips blood offering to no one,
amoral music. No one crosses a river twice.
It's common sense: don't look back
once you've made the great leap
over the waters, *alea iacta est*

don't ever look back.

Following the song ever inward.
It's a labyrinth. Walls twist
in scraps of ghost. It's all brick,
all mortar, all memory and wasted life.
All that will never pulse except in here,
in the gullet

o hungry Hecate
will you never be sated? Give my soul
back to me. I cannot live without it,
I am not one of the living,
I wander lost and do not breathe -

if only I
could become whole! For these jewels
and bricks are nothing, even your magics mighty gods.
If I remained here I would not be whole -
my wound drips even now
thus give it to me, my life, I find Lethe abhorrent,
the sword which severs is my only cure -
offering of my wasted life:
sever me an exit from myself...

    She hears thunder and music.
It's memory that draws her back, seduced.
Memory of a silver chord, a love undying
(*o I will follow you yet, anywhere you will,*
I am yours not mine) What
is death's claim, next to desire's?
Even Persephone, even Dis, can bow. They know
their own kind. Aphrodite has a home here
when she visits. The newly dead,
like gods, must answer the call of pain and prayer.
A small grace, from the gods.

    Ascension
the choir of voices
dead: like angels. Winged. Pain gives wings
to the dead. So slow, victory's beating wings
are slow next to despair's bronze chariot,
why can he not speed the triumphal orchestra
to his own pace? Must pain take forever?
He has courted death so long.
He searches and searches, but nowhere

does he see his soul in the twisting hall.
Only echoes of her hands on his head;
the hands of a priestess
or a deity. Dead memories. All he sees

   is a dead leaf

   falling slowly through winter wind.
First snowfall. Laughing flakes. The joy
of the eternal gods. He is alive,
he who has bartered his life for song
with his soul as coin; pleading,
even though his soul is long lost,
his soul that he will never hear echo
but in mirror's perversion –
a joke, meant for himself
alone:

   o why must I always look back?
For the soul is her own; she keeps her own mysteries,
she mocks me. I will never reach her being,
I will never own my soul.

Garden

Long past midnight, in these enclosed walls
it's always been three in the morning. It's no time
for any person to be awake, to be kept awake
by any force of habit or circumstance or nature
- and no person is awake here, no one but I
in this forest of roses and sweet night blossoms.
The scent is narcotic, all white petals
and honey. It suggests dreams. There are poppies, too.
Somewhere in a tree, where blossom the beginnings
of ripe figs, or perhaps olives, a nightingale sings: *tereu, tereu...*
Sings so sweetly. I should be asleep, but sleep eludes me.
On such a night it is easy to think that I might
never sleep again, there will never be a night
such as this. How could anyone really sleep
on such a night, when the nightbird cries just so,
when the blossoms are so impossibly scented with fragility?

Examine the rose. I have touched its petals hundreds of times,
tonight. Velvet red petals, wine petals, unfolding slowly
in the night. I have stroked these roses so many times,
becoming one with their delicate majesty, understanding.
Insomnia, after all, brings clarity...I see the thorns,
blunt, but sharp as razors in the ideal, glaring, reminding.
Petals do not come without thorns. The red of the rose

is the flush of blood. It is the way of things.
Such sharp stars, relentlessly sane echoes of a silver city
once upon when, a pattern that wants madness but is really
only mad in its logic. Truth itself is mad. Oh, why
must everything be so clear! I would rather be deluded.
I would rather be blind, in a valley of the blind.

I can see the stars, the roses, the cold rocks upon which
the night is reflected, I can hear the sighs of the nightbirds
and of sleeping children who sleep the sleep of the innocent.
I can see how this will end. I can see the question, written
out in stars, the question which I once asked, which I long ago
forgot, but never really forgot; the question that you ask in your addresses,
gazing at me with your uncomprehending eyes. I can see it
in the folds of rose petals, in the discreet thatch of hedges,
the sway of leaves on the slightest breath of wind.
There is really only one answer. The only remaining question
is whether one will accept it with grace, or with rebellion.
The answer remains the same...You cannot hear it, unless perhaps
in the fitful dreams that come to you in sleep, but it is there,
as relentless as tide. As the soft, muffled sound of beating wings.
As the approach of dawn. Oh, why this cruelty? Grace is cruel.
The coming of dawn is no comfort.

The Snake

They would blame it on me: the heat of the sun, bearing down
on their hot sweaty necks.
The pain of muscles aching from overwork,
the death of their children
and all the blood spilled onto dirty rushes.
They always wanted someone to blame.
Their eyes, when they sought me -
shifty, restless with the desire
to disobey. Children with their hands
itching to get caught in the sweet jar.
When had it ever been different?

I saw it coming, of course,
and I told him that no good would come of it
but naturally he refused to listen to reason.
So there I was, sent to the garden
on a ridiculous mission of goodwill.
Get to know them, he said. They'll grow on you.
He never listens to my advice.
Those vipers were bad from the beginning;
beautiful, oh yes, they had his face and eyes
and his fair speech and long limbs,
to look at them was to love them,
how could one not fall in love?

The woman, ah, she with the tumbling frothing curls,
sweet waterfall of gold glinting reflected in the pool...
But they were made of clay. Clay cracks.
It oozes in the rain, and if tempered in heat,
it shatters when you drop it. It has its uses,
but it's still clay.

Like all parents, he had eyes only
for his children. Who was I to argue?

We met for the first time in the olive orchard, she and he and I,
she lusting after my white skin
and wondering whether she could touch
the muscles on my alabaster legs,
he thinking of what it would be like
to have wings of his own,
to fly and touch the face of the sun.
They were brown and soft. They were
people of the earth, and the air fascinated them,
for it was an element that had never been theirs.
They could not see beyond their world
and they tried so hard - they did not even see
the shimmering green leaves swaying
in the breeze, the green olives
begging to be sampled, the impossible softness
of soil. They glanced at the deepening blood-crimson twilight
and then looked away. They wanted to see
stars in my eyes. Please, murmured the woman,
please give me a star, and let me name it
after myself. Let me keep a star.
It would be such a lovely thing to keep.

They were always like that with me.

No, I said, I have something better.
For that was not what they wanted.
I saw even then that my stars,
my sphere, my music, would never be enough.
I sang to them and it bored them
unless they heard their names in the chords.
They would not even want to breathe
in that dark, silver temple of sound and light.
So I pointed them in the right direction,
the way they so obviously wanted to go.
There, that's where your real interest lies.
You see those golden apples? And that was it.
It took no more convincing. And in truth
(have I ever lied, save by withholding truth?)
I gave them exactly what they desired.
Like their father, they have children,
little copies of them that are perfect and pretty
until they crack. They are extremely fond and proud.
Have you ever seen a woman's face
during childbirth? She screams, she curses,
she swears she hates God and the whole male race,
and then she has her child in her arms
and even if it doesn't have all ten toes
or fingers, she still sees nothing but her child.
It's all because of me. It's the pain of bearing
that makes her realize how much she loves her progeny.
It's sending her son to bed without dinner
because he played truant,

then wondering where she ever went wrong
to produce such a child, that reminds her.
She can't turn her child out. The son is hers.
And in that moment, she knows divinity.
I've given her a small gnosis.

It's what they want. Of course,
when I don't give them what they want
that's when they complain. They
complain about me. They complain about him.
As if either of us had anything to do
with the randomness of life going wrong!
They're such typical masochists:
they're only happy when they are feeling pain
that they asked for. They always want control.
They never want to see
just how much work goes into
maintaining the atmosphere for suffering.

He doesn't love me anymore. At least,
he doesn't talk to me very much.
The last time I saw him
we were walking in the desert,
he trying to explain his irrational love
for this venomous offspring,
I trying to get him to see sense.
Let them go, I said. They never listen
to us. They only hear what they want to hear.
Let them grow up, and bail themselves out
of whatever trouble they've got themselves into.
We quarreled. He walked away

without saying a word of farewell.

I was left holding the apples.

Did he notice that I cried at his death,

or attended his funeral, leaving a perfect rose

at the mouth of the sepulchre?

I gave him a rose, and a diamond

that I made out of my tears.

I'll never know if he liked my gifts,

we don't speak anymore. I try not to watch,

I can't help being myself, he wouldn't have it

any other way anyhow; and he can't help

being himself. My stars are lonely without his voice.

They've been silent for years.

STRUCTURES

Jacqueline: Linked Haiku

Brown eyes blink
in darkness. A direct approach.
Bold eyes, shy hidden form.

Her red hair in mine.
Her tongue snakelike flickers.
Two other shades of fire -

pointed breast tips
taste like apricots - sweet, pale flesh.
Moon on an orchard.

(Orchard trembling
in petal-fall. Soft voice
of nightbird.
Lady sings the blues).

Cassandra: Linked Haiku

From the first thunder of spring
bloom roses:
the night petals of longing

I tilt my head back
to slake my thirst with warm rain -
I am lightning-soft.

The roses burn, a
flaming sacrifice to
the goddess of my want.

The rains have gone, and
you with them: memory lies
on the roses - dew.

A kestrel flew away -
why can I not spread my wings
and follow the wind?

Cold and desolate
blows the wind from my city
to your far abode.

Cassandra: More Haiku, Somewhat Linked

A cat cries in want
of a lover; would that I felt
the sweet stroke of your hand!

Your honor lies in my hands,
where you have placed it.
Why is it so sharp?

We met in battle;
what folly, to engage in war
without armor!

Beyond the cherry blossoms,
a stable tree's trunk:
ah! mad, fleeting spring!

The cup brims over;
the sweet wine of love's promise -
my parched throat cries thirst.

The veil is lifted.
Now truly I see the face
of living beauty!

Cassandra: Unlinked Tanka

Autumn now is here;
the leaves fall to frosted ground
and no lovers play
within the cherry orchard.
The time for blossoms is past.

*

Behind the rice paper screen
two kimonos fall.
Furtive the whispers,
but how delicate the hands
of my lady when we tryst!

*

I once loved a butterfly.
She flitted about
my garden, touching
the flowers with her beauty.
She has flown to other flowers.

*

I remember you,
love, the long springtime we shared,
the gazing fondness,
but also the bitter nights.
I shall let the seasons turn.

(Another villanelle)

We romped in waves of moonlit black
   And swallowed the lake to take our fill.
   You fastened my cape behind my back.
   I prayed on my knees as my legs went slack.

   Deep kisses went deeper than my will
   And I succumbed to your attack
   With a hunger that startles me still.
   (But could I not drown, to take my fill?)

   Nights later, held on my back,
   By some strange tremor that put me still,
   I writhed in the cuffs that held me slack
   And laughed in the face of the attack

   Drinking in the autumn, my mouth goes slack
   At what the memories call back -
   The things I did in autumn
   That I might take my fill!

It Is The Beginning Of The End

It is the beginning of the end
of the beginning; my soul is held
and bound; torn, that it will mend.

Your eyes are dark, and hungry.
I stare at you. I know full well
that this is the beginning of the end.

My wrists. You pin and pull
on strings that bind a dying heart.
My soul is held that it will mend.

I feel your need, a sucking mouth
that beckons like the void;
it is the beginning of the end

as, twisted like rope, we fall. Desire is dark,
sharp as steel; compelling as fate.
My soul is torn - but it will mend.

This hunger for *life*. Giving no release
unless we lose ourselves – oh, hold!
It is the beginning of the end.

My soul is torn that it will mend.

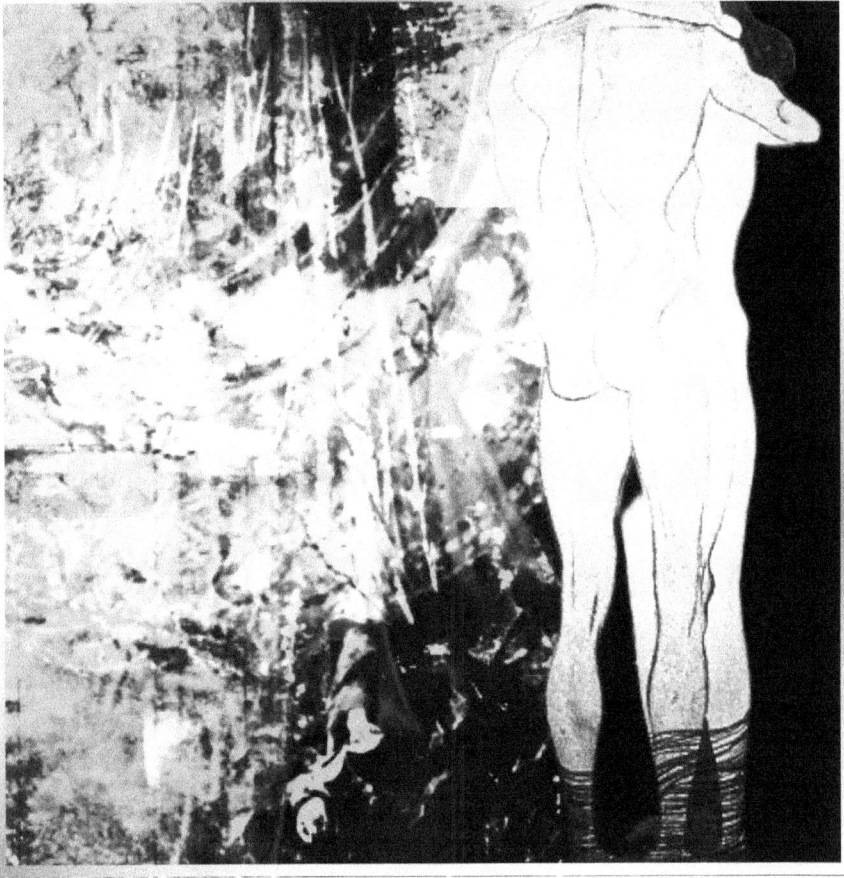

On A Theme by Jaufre Rudel

When now the days are long in June
I love to hear the dial tone distant,
and when the sound must die - too soon -
I dream about a love as distant;
Deep in my worst debts I am drowned.
Adverts for calling cards abound,
and warm me no more than winter snow.

But I believe that the airlines one day
will let me see this love that's distant.
(Ah, for one good call, my lot, I pay
with double bills, since he's so distant)
Would as an heiress I were clad,
and with a hundred grand to add:
I'd tell my creditors which way to go.

What pleasure it would be to pay,
Good God! the bills to that place far distant;
for when I've pleased, I'd often stay
on the telephone lines with my love far distant -
What sweet discourses will abound,
when near the distant love is found:
and may the phone bill once again be low...

Love has no joy when I must stay
and pay for this love that is so distant.
Such postage, fees, would keep away
all but the dauntless from their love far distant.
So helpless am I to my debt
that I am tempted my pants to wet.
To end this plight, I'd distant go;

The industry has fashioned this, I'd say.
It's conspired to keep my good credit far away.
Oh hear me cry, and don't delay
but give me yet my traveler's discount -
In such sweet bliss (I'd barely stand!)
would I be, if I could leave this land -
and go where no collectors know!

This Is Just To Say (for Emma)

This is just to say
that since March
I have been staring
at your picture
to the point
where I have become virtually useless

thank you
for your cheeks
your stormy-grey eyes
your breasts
and your passionate noises

(the plums weren't so bad, either)

One Final Song of Experience

With profuse apologies to William Blake

I am a little bolt
I hold two parts together
I am made so that I work
In any kind of weather

I am inspected by a crew
They see that I am strong;
They touch my parts and peer at me
And see my neck is long

If I am good then I am passed;
A company mark I wear.
My inspector was recently hauled away
For screwing me into their ear.

Noli Me Tangere

(in reply to Sir Thomas Wyatt)

Noli me tangere.
I lie alone,
my heart is of stone;
do not touch me.
Dull poisoned tips
pierce those whose guard slips -
best let me be;
my face may be fair
but wise men beware.
Noli me tangere.

I Have Walked the Night-Lit Ways

I have been one acquainted with the night - Robert Frost

I have walked the night-lit ways
Past pine trees (climbing the wind-whipped gloom)
The embrace of their limbs a myrrh-scented tomb;
The evergreen hall where lovers cry,
An evergreen crypt where lovers lie.
I have padded the husky hills
Amid the bodies of stricken leaves
And followed the current of where the wind willed
And soared on the swells of where the fog heaved.
I have spoken with singing Sidhe
Drunken on rhyme and faery mead –
The barrow lady who sang with me
Poured waters of life to quench my need.
I have learned the ways of mist,
Paid heed to words the adder hissed,
And heard the veins of those I kissed.
I have, wolf-wise, howled the moon's praise –
I have walked the night-lit ways.

It Was Dark In the Night

It was dark in the night
when Fate took my hand;
The shutters protested
As a wind swept the land.

We skimmed out the door,
Two leaves on the gust;
Blown on by Force,
Abandoned to Trust

Fate asked me then
If I longed to be free -
I stared through the wind -
As she stared through me -

Giving no answer
But blinded by night,
I gave up my wings
To our circling flight;

Gave up my wings
my trembling wrists -
My neat fingers clenched
In trembling fists -

Husks of frail leaves
on the cold autumn breath
Go spinning alone
Against the white rose of Death

But such warmth in the chill!
and so sweet to be blown!
In the palm of a goddess
I spin not alone -

The Forging of the Grail

Burning fire, then, in the cauldron,
until out of the crucible, into the mold,
outpouring of the spirit into a shape
not unlike a Grail; made firm in the cold,
you wait for the hands of your maker.
How premature was that sigh of relief!
I have known fire so many times
that my fire markings defy belief.
I have cried for mercy in that dark hour
just before dawn, and been denied.
Mercy's not a thing for grails.
You'd shake if you were untried,
says the sadistic Smith, and you'd snap.
Better to snap now before the trial.
And he sings as he pumps the bellows,
and choking on my black bile
I try to intone a descant. My high note
rings out in darkness, my soul withstands,
I curse the pain and protest
as a Grail forms under the goldsmith's hands.

Wild Blow The Winds On This Black Night (The Maenad)

Wild blow the winds on this black night -
laughter shrieking within my dumb ears.
A baying of dogs, the sound of horns, the mad light
of the moon blazing empty and fierce:
Here is where I make my halt. My white feet
writhe on the grass, seeking a soothing peat.
The raw soles kiss blade. White burns red.
It is a nowhere-space to which I have fled.
And the god is about: which mercy will he bring,
the ecstasy of the arrow, the sweet death's bed?
This mad poet would sing.

Death is in every gift. Do not fight
the glance, the sharp kiss, the sweet metal tears
of rain falling on midwinter's blight -
The soft sobbing patter is all the soul hears.
Dark plains of the night, where my heart might beat
from its chest; throbbing; where my mouth might eat
yet stranger foods: nectar, ambrosia, toadstool-bread,
accepting dark hell with delighted dread.
Love of my masked lord is a frightening thing.
The ground near my feet is soaked where I've bled;
This mad poet would sing.

This hell token coiled about my neck (Now invite
what's beyond the mask to the body mask-worn)
Here in this wood, mosses of malachite
entwine tressy roots along granite spears.
A gasping coitus is what makes me complete;
thick honey drips, mingling with the blood at my feet.
I give up myself. My light glows where I spread,
my hair tosses - and an ancient figurehead,
an oracle, a wild prophet, I scream - The moon is bleeding
but none perceive. These words stay unsaid.
This mad poet would sing.

ENVOI

This blind rapture is sweet -
My blinded eyes see what day-bound eyes dread,
Paths seldom trod are the ways that I tread,
Following stars to dark wakening -
My submission is serene. This horn at my head.
This mad poet would sing.

For the Holly King

Before the last gasp of muddy cold
spreads foggy against the winter's sky
and the frost comes to harden the ground
and whitens the twitching, rat-colored grass -
before the snow pellets fall on all things dun
and mutely, calmly, bring winter on -
Not first the moon, turning her sideways smile,
shrugs herself into her cloak of night;
while all the world's stars wink on and out
and march into the advancing light -

The winter's fire burns out on the hearth,
juniper smoke curls away into vines;
ashes settle in the pit to earth.
In ashes of grey I call forth a form:
lines marching in columns traced by youth,
an aging god of an aging race;
and exhumed, my hands grey with the ashes
of gods and myth, time and space
laid out in the sarcophagi of library casings -
time gathers in and grows old.
Winter congeals on my hands, in ash, to dust;
I toss wood on the embers, against the cold.

Alba

In waiting for the loved so far away
We cry to the night (how long are nights in May!)
We cry to night, for the pleasures that she brings.
Pleasures are twilight, fleeting and grey -
   oy Deus, oy Deus, de l'alba tan t'ost ve! -
We dwell in night. Life's many springs
give life a life by meanings of things.
In meanings, in dreamings, breathe mortal clay:
in the valleys of blind men, are one-eyed kings...
We dwell in night and dream of day.
The body's a prison; our souls fly away
to the arms of their marble god of desire.
But hell sends wind to her souls led astray.
And fear no pain and fear no fire:
If love is flame, we build our pyre
though our cinders cry; our ash is grey.
We dream of dawn and to what we aspire,
And we dream of heaven's circling gyres
living sweet hell; caught in loves wings,
The day interrupts, demanding its way -
Can one consent to the pain dawn brings?

All dreams must end, all nights go grey.

Is It Love That Possesses Me To Write

Is it love that possesses me to write,
or lust? Surely in the depths of my loins
burns poetry; and in that cauldron, where joins
spirit of longing and essence of painful sight,
is the inspiration found only in desire.
Yet it is something else that makes me strive
to create poetry for you, to make words come alive
in hymns of adoration. This lyric, you inspire.
It is yourself that gave the gift of holy flame to me.
I strain to show my gratitude, for you to see
that in my striving to do honour, there is only love.
Lust fuels the fire that burns my sleepless night;
Love purifies the flame, and sees me fit to write.

Sonnet for Marie

All I can commit to paper is your hair,
the sweetness of your flesh and blood;
I would rather capture inner beauty, not stare
at the physical shadow of where you stood.
Yet I am helpless. I only obsess
on your perfect bosom, your catlike moves,
the shadowy form that I long to caress,
but surely your soul is what my soul loved?
Our conversation was delightful, our love as well
and if this fragility of feeling disproved
its reality, nevertheless, it was in love that I fell.
Your absence is something of which I'm all too aware -
yet all I can commit to paper is your hair.

Love's Place

Is love in a glance,
    A passionate sigh?
    The ache in the heart
    The dilated eye
    The hungering need
    that wakes in the blood –
    A loud ecstasy
    Between should and could

    Is love in cold hands
    That reach for each other
    The embrace in the dark
    One heart for another
    The firmness of soil
    The patience of sea
    The eternal hope
    that tomorrow will be

    Love is forever
    At least for a day
    A dangling prize
    Not quite far away
    Love's beyond gold
    though wanting will do –

Love can rend hearts.

Wanting hurts too.

For Arthur, After Our Parting

You loved me, you said, because I was strong
   (Though some would say arrogant,
   or perhaps even heartless.)
   Or was that the reason why? You gave
   No reason, really; save that I played along
   With the game, the grand façade,
   and played with panache
   (Though some said otherwise,
   my candour being far too artless.)

   You loved me, you said, for my mind.
   (At least its many twists and turns,
   the way it took its perverse pleasure.)
   You gloried in the dance we made,
   The steps and feints, the unkind way
   I fenced each encounter...Was I so awful?
   My fists were always gloved in velvet,
   ready to stroke where I might strike
   (Though – only at my own leisure.)

   You loved me once, yet now no more.
   (Indeed I must be graceless,
   certainly I am far too artless.)
   Why the game? I have walked brambled footpaths

on old untided trails, to the shore.

Its cliffs were pale, and seductive;

But I, mistress of seduction, pay little heed

to the charms of oblivion. I am immune,

having become cold; perhaps even heartless.

Sorrow, My Heart

Sorrow, my heart,
For summer has flown.
True loves must part.
Sorrow, my heart;
The lilacs they wither
and true love must part -
It is all gone.

Sorrow, my heart,
For summer has flown.
True loves will part;
sorrow, my heart.
Cold breathes the wind.
What now is my own?
For the wind is unkind.

Sorrow, my heart,
For summer has flown.
True love must part,
and sorrow's my heart -
Now flies my art
To chase leaves that have blown.

Sorrow, my heart.

Summer has flown.

A Triolet

He greets me in state
Says he – Miaow –
The world I relate;
He greets me in state.
My victuals he ate,
No food have I now.
He greets me in state,
Says he, Miaow.

WEEPING, ANARCHIC APHRODITE

The Precipice

Here we stand on the brink of the precipice
awaiting – what? A star in the East?
some other portent? No matter. We wait.
I touch you, my hand piercing
the layers of dermis and epidermis
to brush the pulsing muscle
that beats the time to your dance.
It throbs against my palm,
warm and vital, thrilling to my touch.
I want to sing.
As if in defense, you clutch at my shadow
refusing to let go, a child holding
a treasured possession.
On the edge of the cliff
we stare at the yawning chasm, hushed,
keening for the music of the spheres.

The Romance of the Switch

O, you are too dangerous for me,
no more slave to me
than I am slave to my better nature.
Your eyes take too much sparkle
as they take pleasure
from inflicting desire upon me.
Your fingers are too ready
to jump and be nimble for me;
And your soul, your soul!
A positive irony that you'd submit to me,
and a positive impossibility.
Insouciant, you lie on my bed of lusts
calling me by my rightful titles –
All the while thinking of painting the ceiling
beige and comparing yourself
to a slab of meat
(you snob, it's probably filet mignon, too)
I eat you without even punishing you
though by now you certainly deserve it...

No. I know who the real master is, here,
and I will not abide it. Do you hear me?
Listen: you will be mine,
even if it means fire and brimstone,

the lash, and lycanthropy itself –
whereby man is changed into dog.
Even if it means that I must submit –
horror of horrors! Did I say that? Alas,
it is too late for me, I can see. Already
I am writing you poetry.

Blood Calls to Blood

Queen of Swords, you come bearing a grail.
What is the meaning of it?
Your suits are blessed confusion.

You appeared in my cards at midwinter.
Since then, I have religiously
avoided sunlight, become deathly afraid
of wood. Once High Priestess, I have become the Fool.

I journeyed to the underworld
in search of a cauldron.
Ceridwen laughed and filled it.
I have tasted of the waters of life;
Three drops of wisdom on my tongue, searing.

Blood calls to blood.
I, the living, crave life. O sweet addiction!
For one more taste of liquid fire
I would brave the Watcher once more.

Eros and Thanatos At the Juncture of Lovemaking

Pictures curl together a locket,
strands of soul untouched by sun;
each to each, held warm to the breastbone, each one.

You in Babylonian sky, hot midafternoon;
you, hurrying to your temple
laden with tablets: grain reports,
taxes, tallies of household slaves.
I crashed into you, aflutter with my perfumed duties;
cuneiform spilled onto the stones
and scurried away in a swarm of wedge-shaped ants.
The blessings of Inanna, I murmured
and then the flood washed us both away
like so much silt from the Tigris

(Had I only known you then)

I would have danced my scarves in the temple moonlight

You in ritual mask, eyes hidden behind goddess;
knowing that the lot has been drawn,
even your daughter, firstborn -

did I protest the sacrifice, my love,
gazing at you with questioning cateyes
to make your needs upset the sacred scales?
I did not. I bowed low, forehead to the ground
that was your goddess feet, and rose
to climb the hill of lava
and sacred death

(Had I only held you then)

We would have commanded the sun to still

In moonlight hot as fire,
an alpine chill breathing jealous cold
at our castle walls;
you are drunk enough to halt in your ghost tale
to slosh against my wife's ear -
I did not challenge you to duel, then;
at least not in earnest. Or to the death.
But I partook of wine and incense
and swore brotherhood by ancient rite -
and the incense smoke curled curls
giving birth to phantoms made of moon, Alby,
to contracts signed in much essence

(Had I not drowned in your seas)

A prodigious poem we would have made, in Attic Greek

The jungle wavers, hot with blood
darkness of sunlight
lust. And your youth in quiltwork,
my friend, all thread embroidery spilling
out of the basket, onto the yellow silk
red of the Asian soil:
your tapestry cried to be unwoven:
How could I refuse Atropos, to hold you yet to me?
Thus I swallowed my jealousy of the shadow lover
and stood in her place, again,
sending you that time to her arms
knowing the whore would have me next.
And I stared scrying into your entrails' weavings,
seeing your soul fly west
on the back of the bird

(Had we not stopped for death)

We would have damned ourselves for eternity some more

You are soul in weavings still,
a cord that braids itself in my hand
to become a Kundalini serpent, unknowing.
Night sky and hot fire from the candles
witness our sacred marriage
our rite of rebirth, our re-remembering
in these bodies warm and masked in love's
bare bones encased in flesh.
Your arms holding me phoenix
in the heart of the hierogram;

Soul strands, links of fire,

passion the outstretched arms of death -

and from your embrace, Mystic Sister,

I draw forth my breath:

I would pray to my muse to teach a scythe to sing

Amor Alchemica

Deep in the stone heart of the forge,
fire leaps a dance to caress the sky.
A breath from the bellows
is the roar of the dragon.
Phoenix rises. Deep in the heart of my brother's eyes
fire leaps a dance, to brush the back
of the spheres.

Phoenix rises, and dances at the third gate.
Cymbals; and the sulphurous smell of sweat.
Deep in the heart of his eyes
my brother's dross is turned to gold;
veiled behind Ishtar's gauze are his mysteries,
but I have pierced beyond. A breath from the bellows.
Phoenix rises, and my brother seeks the fire.
The veil is pierced; the philosopher's stone is found,
and the third gate is breached.

The phoenix rises to dance
the music of the spheres. Deep in the heart
of the flames, the planets are still.
A breath from the bellows. The roar of the dragon
is my brother transformed
in phoenix flight. The veil is pierced.

We two are one

in the embrace of the gods.

Summer At Autumn's Fall

Meeting the summer king in the glade. Here it is crux of autumn;
leaves red and gold fall down into the fire circle.
Feeling him enter me. I, the novice, have come forth
to be made woman. His fingers are on my lips,
hushing me with sweet furtive dew
that might be his ecstasy, and might be mine;
so I drink it in, drink the wine held
to my open mouth, taste the arrival
of his pleasure as I feel the leaves,
their soft rustle falling on my nearly naked skin.
Sips of sunlight. In this circle of sunlight
a shaft of light touches me at the crescent.
I am a vampire, I protest. I am a creature
of blood and shadow, I hide in graveyards
for fear my darkliness will be hunted and staked –
But he holds me in the sun, until I consent
and allow the sun to enter my gasping flesh.
It feels exquisite.

Instrument

You are so silent

your weight on me a warmth,
passion wrapped about you in a golden halo

The only sounds you make are breaths,
little winds; breaths, and the occasional murmur,
a consecrated fragment of ritual and sex -

it is I who must scream out for you
wailing like a gypsy violin, a Devil's daughter,
strung all of taut catgut and hollow spaces

music made from fire and longing
rips from my body

to defy the silence of night

Amazing To The Clear Waters

Amazing to the clear waters of my desire
that the absence drunk in
fills to flood:
that in this nothing
of relationship's strings
the heart beats strained,
vestigial voices of swans aching to trumpet
a love that blooms well into the dark never
and in the absence of you
the zero is yet consuming

Stanza

(no working title)

Still the night, while in cold snowfall
Stars shine, to reach the diamond earth -
in such pale heat is my spring.
Distant, a small still point, dancing.
Distant is the music of the spheres.
Distant, and far.
Ah, love, that yours should be
such a wintry sun!

In the Wake of Conflagration

In the wake of conflagration
how my heart is spitted from my chest
still beating for you
and amazing the carnal effect
that in pain and out of flesh
this is where I remain
oh – and how sweet in substance
do I burn beyond desire
alive in a feeling
that cannot be described in vain
as love

The Tender Danger In My Eyes Seeks Your Flame

The tender danger in my eyes seeks your flame;
I am afraid to touch you; I fear to look too long,
for I would put my own eyes out –
There is too much danger in beauty. Where
is the destiny in fire, that calls me
like a sacrificial moth? My wings of searing soul
have become powder. Only the wind makes me hover,
at your bed, by your side, over your shoulder...
I dare not trust the wind, it breathes too hard;
I dare not trust the hot exhalation torn
from your mouth during lovemaking;
when ashes are blown away, there remains nothing
but a dry husk of an exoskeleton,
inching feebly to the light. You burn me,
my love burns me, I live in constant fear of immolation.

From the Foam

In the unholy terror of this distance
(how cruel the gods!) – yet still I can
reach your trembling body,
your sweat libating the sheets,
your limbs straining against the leather straps –
and the muffled noise of your distress
floats past my ears like a sad, half-heard
wail. In the distance, the pounding
of the ocean, fists against a pillowed surface,
your entire being encompassed
in the echo of the conch

that I clasp to my ear,
that I caress like a lover's body.
The sea always echoes in a rush of blood.
I can almost touch you,
past these waves. I would be dead
not to hear the rushing of the sea.

No Magic Philtre Have We Drunk

No magic philtre have we drunk,
no crazy coincidence have we come through.
No notorious circumstance have we yet endured.
No night's blindfold has yet covered either
of our sets of eyes,
no masquerade has made our dance complete.
No stars have appointed our paths to cross,
our paths wound parallel along their own axis -
and were they to cross, it would be
no remarkable thing.
No crystal castle, no mountains mist,
no consecration of blood -

and yet! how haunting is the image
of your midnight eyes, nearly black,
black as the cave, flickering shadows illusions
displaying dreams against stone and earth
off some great, unimaginable height.

How desperate the passion in your limbs
your shuddering ecstasy, fear joined
at desire's hips, how bewitching
your noble attempt to hold still
in the face of the willow lashes.

Your suffering seems that of a hero,
or of a god. Even these signs alone
seem enough, despite the silence
of the oracles. Enough. You possess me.
My soul must hence see a different dawn.

Elegiac

I.

The black crinoline
of oblivion
brushes its tresses against her eyes;
she floats. And her body
is a ship
sailing on to the west.
A taste of wine sour in her mouth.

Waves of night lapping at the shores
rise on a tide:
engulfing night.

When the sun rises to illuminate
her unconscious parallels,
harsh rays on night-worn skin,
the disappointment she feels
is a still content -
a content silent as marble.

Her mouth held open
until the poison creeps out
in a spittle of dawn.

Death will not be hers, this day.

II.

My beloved,

How to tell you that I am leaving? I cannot. My body will have to speak for me - not my spirit's surcease in death, that magnetic quest...But I do not really want to be free! I am confused, I no longer understand whether my death will free me or condemn me to an eternity of you. I long to ask you these things, oracle to omniscient, but you are silent. Only my heart speaks to me in these strange mists, writing like a restless python. Ah! half the hour is past! 'twill all be past anon! Oh God! In the wake of the sun's desertion, the only embrace remaining is that of darkness!

III.

How she clings to her illusions!

(I clung to him,
then, my living god;
barbiturates and antihistamines,
painkillers and garlic wine,
and too much absinthe
made a steamy miasma
in the confinement of his arms.

I did not tell him
upon waking, nor in the midst

of that final act of desire
that I had taken an overdose;

merely that I wanted to die.

Life without him would not be life,
but a living undeath,
a hell without a sun.)

Perched openly on the tripod
in expectation - but no visions come,
only the empty caress
of the unfulfilled morning.
And all that come to her are methods:
knives, ropes, liebestod,
ways to ease the crossing

to let go of the life
that she had so begged for.

(I wanted him so badly;
I knew this was the end,
the point of no return,
and I wanted to make love to him
before I ended my slavery...

That word! you cry. You never want
to hear it spoken aloud. Nor did I,
nor did he - we do not like to hear
the naked truth, that we are slaves
to our bodies, to our passions,

we dream of escape.
Is it tragedy that death eluded me?
Mad sybil of a rejecting god)

    She feels her mortal coil
clench in fruitless defiance.
And yet, she cries out

    (*don't leave! don't let me go, don't let me go*)

    only to curse when the drug haze comes
to fetch her, that she is denied
the final darkness, the one last adventure -
that she turns coward in the end,
and asks leave of the man
she mistook for a god. Knowing
that it will never be, that there is no release
there is never a release

    She is given a sprig of moly
for her two useless ferry coins.

IV.

    Drifting on the waves,
down the abyss
that somehow never has a bottom;
past white statues.

(*Is it like this,*
in death's other kingdom?
Waking alone)

The very sun is fractured,
the light strange and fleeting
in that shimmering place -

A dark dream,
waves of silver.
Alone in the temple of night,
she allows the wood of the boat
to bite her naked knees

And this is her new world.
The gods that she would worship
are made of alabaster

(*Lips that would kiss*
form prayers to broken stone)

She leaves her offering
at the feet of her statue;
an offering of her body,
herself to herself.
It is the final adventure:
one last drink from the river of knowledge.

How can she smile,
abandoning her very self?

Courtship of the abyss,
chthonic Hecate smiles fangily
behind a bouquet of anenomes

   o run slowly
horses of night!
must the empty dawn
reach for her lips
with fingers of sickly roses once more?

   (She cries there on the shore,
for her fallen god:
cries for the white statues,
for the hollow heap of woman
left at night's shore.
So might Persephone have cried
against the streaming pomegranate)

   The axe never falls
but at the motion of her own hands -
cold smiling day
parting the curtain, at last

  (at her consent)

   Death is of white stone, chalcedon
to the carbon of Eros
Death will not take the mortal, now.
Only the surface remains.

Lines Written at the Beginning of Spring

Ex profundis, the bright-piercing blades
   beyond gold, beyond silver,
beyond any deeply-held colour
of earth or ore or bone-knowledge: calling sweetly
of childhoods, clover, and bare feet -
sunlight shining, an angelic wing
pure in space, warm and nectarine,
aurora and lucifer, motes dancing
in remembrance of that sudden spring
rising from the east

touch me and shatter me, oh beauty of sunlight!

My sweet, you for whom I have lusted
and, lusting, died in shame for lust,
fill me. Already I can feel need
making dust of my clay. A breath
scatters me like leaves.

Only the blood yet lingers, reluctant,
congealing on the threshold of evaporation
like the pools of dusk. Shadows lurk,
waiting to drown.

August

Summer is flaming out;
I live in fear.

Already I feel the sun's indifference
destroying my inner night;
my every step
is a little death.

Already the winds howl laughter
at my straw ideals.
I have heard twigs snap,
at night,
outside my window –
I am afraid.

The skies are full of storms,
protesting. I can hear your voice
moaning in my ears;
the sound is like death –

O chide my coward soul
for weeping at autumn's advance!

Love Poem

Lessons learned on a cold winter night,
wind driving rain patters against glass.
Take this cup from me. It boils,
the burden of a holy grail, a sacrament unpassed,
the sacred burden unwanted. This cup
that is my destiny. I crawl
across carpeted floor, my flesh
a gleaming moon-white
against the golden halo of candle,
and my aloneness is more a burden
than any fire or grail.

*

I want your hands on me.
This I know, that your square spatular palms
mean more to my pilgrim skin
than any meaningless litany. My flesh,
burning, flickers in the sudden cold shock
of pain. These hands, beautiful mystic brother,
are all that hold my shivering soul
steady, against the pull of the void.

They are a fire against darkness,
Promethean and priestlike.

*

Offertorium. This is the part
where the priest sings praise to Dionysos
and leads the goat to death and Olympus.
I bow my head and kiss the consecrated blade –
my blood crying for release. This is how
the goat must feel, consenting to its sacrifice,
willing, warm, liquid.
Your shaft inside my body
is a searing fire. It is burning and need,
embodied, the sweetest pain
that ever you could give.

Another Fragment

My coming shakes me –
like a myrtle struck –
and into your mouth, to
the very winds I moan
percussive breath. The wind carries
me into the heart of thunder.

(Your face in repose, image
of a sleeping god.

A heaven after the storm.)

A Taste of Pomegranate

Where are the fruits? The trees wait,
impatient, and all around the angry drone
of a thousand desperate wasps: autumn is dying.
O come to me, come to me,
the grasses are sere with wanting,
my feet are cracked by clay
and all around me haunts the memory
of green pastures, a more sealike sky
(you commanded the lambs to gambole for me,
that spring)
    The river flowed with honey
and the wind was our friend -
why are you not here?

The memory of a missing spring:
we were drunk on moonlight,
we held a Bacchanale
and ran drunk and raging in the collegiate streets.
Our feet pounded the cobblestones,
pursuing wild places.
I remember the ivy. I can still taste
delirium's ferment on my tongue.

I cannot believe that you are gone.

Let the snow fall and cover cracked clay,
it will not reach my buried soul
until the full moon forces time
to reverse its thread. Let it freeze over.
Let me be a sobbing tree,
naked in the wind. Spring is gone,
and with the flowers I.
Never to return. I have eaten my season.

Rhapsody On the Art of Memory

I cannot sleep.

The wind laughs too loud.
The bed's too warm for my quartered self,
A thousand displayed images mean nothing
to me - I am alone, and fitful, and hollow,
Too sick for sleep. I am this night -
cold soul, black heart, blind sight -

The willow whips the window glass
in a lover's fit. I need your hands,
I cannot sleep. Your life, free of mine,
has forgotten me - I am my own
and I lie crumpled.
I fantasize an abandoned doll.

(My sleepless eyes see laughter on each wall)

Two down, one to go -
three is the charm that binds
and I avoid the third. I've been mastered enough.
My illness burns when I cannot sleep,
it askes me - catechismically - am I not my own?
It sneers. I long to fly.

Laughing on glass panes,
The rain splatters like mad tears:
weeps with my zeroic soul
on its void of fears -

An abandoned mask -
a powerless thing -
a white snow owl without wings -
my dreams strangle me where I lie,
not needing sleep to take me where they will.
I am an ourobouric glyph. Self-eating,
I curl unseen.
My joy needs so little to go where it has been -

My bed is too large, I cannot sleep.
Pictures are poor company to keep.

Fallen Angel

Into the air we rose, your firey wings beating
a cadence of sublime passion.
Feathers of flame licked my face.
I arched back to offer my throat
and saw acres of clouds
in an infinite field of blue.
My life gushed into your eager mouth.
Spent, I slumbered in your arms,
dreams of the heavens fluttering
behind my eyes.
I lived for your breath.

And how many of us know
what it is to be loved
by an angel? The desire,
the pure fire of embodied thought
is more consuming than any earthy hunger.
You spoke to me in music;
I replied with cacophany,
unable to reach the pinnacles
of your ideals.

When you let me fall,
the sun scorched my flesh,

reminding me of pleasures lost.

TABLETS

The Three Ages of Poetry

First there's the rhyme.
Its onset is early – perhaps encouraged
by the books that say poetry is
"a gift of watermelon pickle"
or something like that. Inspired,
we write lyrics to the rain,
how raindrops are blue, and clouds are grey,
and I love you God and now I'll go play!

That ends with puberty, thank heavens,
though puberty has its own drawbacks.
Namely: Jim Morrison and Sylvia Plath.
Where else would all those feelings go
if not in verse? Without poetry
where would we put our suicides,
our lost loves, our tragic family lives
and why we hate out parents?
We'd fall. We'd be like small Satans
and fall to our recreational chemical experiments, burning.

Fortunately, college intervenes
(for those of us who are lucky enough
to go on to college – most do –
we are, after all, talking about

the garden-variety, white-middle-class
poet) and we receive new life.
We write, not about suicide and smelly
teen spirit, but about ISSUES.
And DEATH. And DEEP THOUGHTS. And SEX.
And everything refers to some other poet
Or
  Has
   A
   Funny shape
Or is strikingly original
Or has the word F#@!
in it.

Some people manage to skip this, though,
and go straight to coffeehouses.
That's called slam poetry.
It's less pretentious
because it yells at more people
and uses the word F#@! a lot more.

It's a wonder we ever get published.

Writer's Block

No more. It is space. It is gone. Gone
is the sweet task of pleasure from here,
on paper, on tongue, and I rock from side
to side, swinging, spasming with my attempts
to reach being, but there is no fruition.
Words trickle from my mouth only barely.
This self died long ago. A heart that does not pump
pushes my pen.

My thirst is excruciating.
Already the universe begins to bleed
into a mouth distended with craving.
I choke on clauses, on sensation.
I have become the point. This is the cost
of not surrendering. The raging on.
I give in and fight possession. Rocking.
Biting empty air. Groaning. Forcing.

Works and Days

For many long months, driven from one philosophical port
to another - between storms, clutching to my bosom
treasured tomes - all these lads between me and the black north wind
admitting somewhere in the laundry list of the canon
that freedom in verse is oxymoronic, better
to be mawkishly Victorian than to admit
an inability to rhyme or mark a beat -
for all these seasons, days and nights
my fingers found no work. My pen and keyboard
glared reproachful. I blamed it on maturity,
the self-consciousness of mediocrity:
Who but an adolescent could think insights
important enough to hear, and who but a genius
could commemorate immortalizing sight and thought
past youth? Hardly I.

And so with this shock of fall fruits, windfallen wordapples,
I ate seeds and was forced to truth.

Eliot I am not, to find a still point in a dance
of violence and communion; nor Swinburne,
passionate and empty jongleur
of perversion and rhyme. My shelves burgeon
with what I am not, and only a few leaves

of anthologized hysterics whisper the source
of my fecundity. My poetic cauldron has other agendae
than ideas.

Words drip from my womb and are soaked up
by scraps of paper. No philosophy but small words
of love or hate, childbirth, housekeeping, hunger
or suicide, to be placed on an altar as offerings
and turned into gods. I do it when the moon is full,
and howl. I am the dirt of the grave
and the sweat of sex. Queen of minutiae,
mother of petty magics, my maidenhead perpetually sacrificed
to rhymeless, meterless phrases. These stillbirths
are all I have; they cavort on undeveloped feet,
attached to me by my withered umbilical cords
of dry ink. This is my art, my magnum mysterium,
all that I have, all that I am.

Death of a Muse

In a heap of old leaves and mulch
and rotting scent of old soil
her red hair trails along the ground
dried spring daylilies in a garden past season.
Her mottled white hand pokes up among the mushrooms.
Somewhere you can see the faded blue
of an old hippie skirt. Words scurry away
when you poke the leaves, from eating the remains
of decomposed chrysanthemums.

Art and Aion

Between rhyme and howl
dangles a fragile world,
a mundane egg of art:
where words dance and display
and are not prose
because prose is not fit
for frame or stage. Rhyme
is a cage, golden and twisted
and beautiful are the birds
that sing on its perch, but it must not ever be forgotten
that birds are beings of wing and air
and quills iridescent.
On the framed stage are birds
which sing from art.
To create a poem one must capture
without taming. One must dance
before the bird escapes
the conjuring hat.

A Literary Prayer

(Written after reading *Eugenie de Franval*)

There is a crash of dead wood.

On this dark and stormy night
inspire me; give me the sweating cold
of these stony walls, the grit
that flies in on the gust. I am dust
and my words, seeds and rot.
I will not last. These my offerings,
tiny and fragile, they must take root
in stubborn soil. Fertilize them.
Give them shape. Twisted they may grow,
but their trunks must be strong.
They must reach through the night.
They must be of their ground.

O you my brother
give me your self. We are one, now -
we who felt ourselves born of soil,
suckled on winter, made love to
by lashing winds, shackled by all our elements.
I will drink of you yet.

The bitter drops scald my throat,
and give deeper notes
to my howl. I cry in pain
and it is artful.

Blood of my blood, I offer you to the storm.

Songs of Summer, Discovered in Autumn

2002 - 2004

The Night the Moon Waltzed With Me

(for Joan Vinge, upon reading *The Summer Queen*)

Stars hung in the garden
icing the trees with lantern light.
The ghost of my longing stepped from the sky.
Her white hair streamed. Her eyes did not see
the vast ocean of space between us;
they saw only the invitation and the dance.

And the silken chords of music
played only for us, rippling like a living tapestry
in the night. Bells chimed.
Who could prefer fear to her touch?
I trembled when I took her hand.

The music of the spheres is inscrutable;
we dance to it, patterning infinity.
The space between is not vast.
It is only uncertain. We glide through
the intimate cosmos, on silver wings,
tangled in our eternal embrace.

For T.B.

I always seem to run into you
when I'm damaged; my bruises thrill
to your touch, and your kisses taste
like the distillation of fermented honey,
making me drunk and warm. The holes
in my body stop bleeding, gape,
mouth strange words I've almost forgotten
how to articulate. You ground in me like lightning,
muttering about how you don't like coming so fast.
We talk more. How little we have in common -
politics, religion, all things of importance left unmentioned
besides the mutual need for balm,
a burning hunger that crops up
when least expected.

To S, my ex

Once again in the ugly grey hours
of the pre-dawn, I dreamed of you:
we quarreled. It was the old
endless discussion, so old that I forgot
what the actual words were,
although I can mouth them easily enough
to myself, a twisted rosary of morbid mysteries.
I would have something different. I am tired of words.

For you, for us, I would have you
mouthless, laid bare, and in my hand
a whip of scorpions. I would that
my fingers clenched a tart knife
soaked in the sour vinegar and piss
of my tears and sweat and forced
ejaculations of reluctant desire;
and that to slash into you, bleed
your venomous welts, until of screams
and blood and passion stains and the sight of me
you were drained dry,
and this mountain of spleen that was us
leveled forever. I would have our desire dead
and walk away without looking back.

And no more words would we have
to say to each other. This disgust eats
at me, weakens me even as I live
on it, gnawing dry crumbs of hate as if
they were manna in a desert. I sicken
of dreams that remind.
The end will be near.

Birth and the Maiden

In the darkness I labored,
there, in the tub, like Tiamat,
whale-like, floundering, confused
by my own lack of reaction.
With the dawn came a twinge
but nothing more - it couldn't
be called pain, exactly - I flopped over
the ball, the chair, praying
to no deity in particular,
reading the daily horoscope
and shrugging off the annoying attentions
of the midwives. They pitted me
when I was too slow; the Nubain
made me smile. And then finally
there was pain - but not
where we'd expected it, oh no,
the pain was in my head,
a fully-armed warrior fighting
to escape. No longer myself,
I cried and fumed and fainted
and woke up strapped to a bed,
immobilized by a needle in my spine.
They might have pierced me to the heart,
but the spine was good enough -

I was in no danger of going anywhere.
The monitor bleeped in the darkness
and informed me of transition.
Sooner or later we'd have to cross over
and it had better be sooner,
for their sake. The nurses were impatient.

It's hard to push when you're staked
to a bed. I tried scrambling to my knees
but there was no room to open my legs,
I might knock something over; no room
to settle my lover on the bed to be
my chair. Supine, indignant, I grunted
and screamed and cursed and scared
the other mothers convalescing
in nearby rooms. It was a relief to everybody
when after a mere three hours
and the head at minus two, I begged for the knife.

No matter how many
are in the operating theatre, how crowded,
it's just you and your words and the thing
waiting to be born, failing to find passage
into the world. The right side of my body
felt the scalding hot touch of the scalpel;
I needed more - more drugs, more help,
more energy. I shook from cold
and inhaled greedily when they put the mask
on my face, sucking oblivion
as if it were sweet lemon phosphate.
Gone: the world winked out at thirteen

or maybe it was seventeen; no matter.
I floated in chaos, dead to myself
and my exposed entrails, and when I awoke
I had a daughter. I do not remember
seeing her. I named her for wisdom.

The first time I saw myself in the mirror,
after I came back, I did not recognize
my own face. I was an alien
with puffed cheeks, bleared eyes, wan skin
like a cadaver. My belly was empty
and hurt where it had been sliced open,
the womb scooped out through ropes of intestine
and cleaned with snow and replaced.
My hair brown and rank and slimy
as guts. My breath grave and hinting
of rot. My ability to create tapestries
from words had left. I watched mute
as my child was brought to my breast,
and wondered that such a dead thing as I
could bring forth life.

Home Brewing

Tonight, after my daughter fell asleep,
I crept down the stairs to watch vampire movies;
I held my breath in terror of her waking hungry
and desperate and unwilling of sleep.
I watched. And after tiptoeing
into the first rainy night of autumn
to retrieve old bills from the maildrop,
I took a funnel, an empty pot, a pair
of old hose, and a bottle
of rotting fruit steeped in wine;
dipping my fingers into the seething mess,
I strained the burgeoning liqueur,
praying that sleeping babies would yet sleep.
I made no noise, and I heard none.
The cauldron of fermenting juice bubbled,
and that quietly.

How amazing to me that now,
well into my third decade,
I dip my fingers into wet, soaked panties,
wiggling the slime, inhaling the sweetness
of festering springs, of rot, and think mostly
of recipes, decantings, and the odious possibility
that I have a vinegar mother instead of brandywine.

That if a moan escapes me (and, God forbid, wakes
the baby) it's the result of a realization
that I added too much fennel.

That years ago,
dedicated in fire and sweat and pain
to a goddess of pleasure I barely knew,
I would never have seen myself in a different kitchen,
tending a different fire,
giving my talents to a religious fervor
quieter, but no less demanding or consuming
for all its absence of pain. Feeding a hunger
I never could have seen.

Going Down

Full fathom five, and farther down
I dive. It is as black as ice
and what lives here creeps, bug-eyed,
white-eyed, phosphorescent oozing
trailing tentacles like hungry weeds.
My lantern here is blind in this depth
where no rays of light make bold
to caress. I wear no suit
and the dead sea licks at my clammy skin.
In primordial chaos eels glide,
mouths beckoning like caverns,
their teeth jewels, little fish
shining. Here is where I go when day
is finished. I am company to monsters.

I've dived here before. This place
is rank with my words. Every wound
sends me here to drown. I dream
in the land of giants, chewing my liver
and breathing in the bile. This cold place
is like nowhere else - its salt is not of life
or anything like life, absinthe's bitter fairy
is sweet to this stream. I suck bones.

O, my hair might be red as flame,
dyed with fire, but I am no phoenix;
I drink blood not fire, I consume,
gorging on hearts and sucking obsession
as if it were cherry filling. Lazarus
might have learned a trick or two
from my leprous hands. I thrash in the water,
seeking my tail, sloughing off my life
and death and humiliation while waiting
for rebirth. I've done this before. I can reach
my depths and bestow on myself
the obscene kiss. My end is my beginning;
I drink to this.

My hairs, like weeds, Ophelia's bitter herbs,
whip, stirring the waters.
The current blinks. On a distant continent
the earth shakes off a coil.

First Frost

The night after Michaelmas we drove
up. My husband left me with the baby
to help with the moving van
in what would, in hours, be home.
The lights were on and my breath
made clouds. It was midnight,
too early to call the utilities.
My daughter could not sleep. She cried
and cried in my arms,
crying "dada!" and "mama!"
nuzzling for warmth. Eventually
sleep took her. I put her in the playpen
so that I could write a poem,
covering her with the afghan blanket
and two velvet shirts.
I considered removing my blazer
or my layered sweater and flannel nightgown
but my teeth chattered.

It is now three in the morning as I write this
on a diaper. I am a devourer.

An Invocation of Waves

I have become the loving goddess
Golden lady, laughter-loving, poor dove,
sea-foamed one, blonde one, dumb one -
because it is a wedding I attend
and a wedding wants a blessing.
I pour the chemicals, gasp, choke,
regard my husband whose oven
makes rubies and diamonds from coal,
and bright dawn from dark.
I remove my flame tresses, cook away
my chemical intelligence. Slowly
my hair turns hideous carrot, radioactive yam.
Beauty emerges with a twist of lung,
head dizzy from fumes. This is the birth
of laughter, this golden hue,
this spun metal the color of a wedding ring,
this ray of dawn's hope born from ashes
and cinders, sulking embers. I am reborn,
faint and raw as bleached bone:
a good omen. Raising high the torch
on hymeneal rites.

Miscarriage

The twinge came that afternoon.
With the spilled blood of the winter sun
came a trickle, then a torrent, blood gushing
warm and wet between her legs.
Finally there was the sickening, faint moment
when the clump appeared: sliding ooze,
a tadpole encased in snotty stuff
and more blood, falling with a loud plop
into the commode.

The doctor told her to collect the specimen.
Even one so young, barely human, would need
examination. What could have caused the poor thing
to collide headlong with fate? She needed to fish it out,
but how? Her dyeing gloves had been used up
with her last root job. Certainly bare hands were out.
She couldn't bear to touch the blood,
the gobs of blood that raised the level of the water
nearly to the brim - at least, that's what it looked like -
and it was a *toilet*, for crying out loud,
she couldn't put her bare hand in a *toilet!*

The scoop sat nearby. It only took a minute
to find a jar; and empty

of all emotion, or treacherous memory
of being almost a mother, she took the handle;
traveling through time to when,
in the third grade, she found the goldfish floating
belly-up in its bowl. How,
dispassionately, she scooped out the orange fish
and bore it to the bathroom.

About the Author

Sera Maddox Drake (seramaddoxdrake.com) fell to Earth several eons ago and skulked around doing odd jobs (trilobite herding, quantum particle illumination, stromatolite swaddling, mayhem instigation, dragon impersonation, peirazomancy, data entry) until they found an opportunity to write a book.

Alternately, they find it both impossible and bizarre to draft an author bio that humble-brags about published writing, literary connections, experience, etc when there is nothing to put on the page, other than "Ooh, look at me! I have a degree, and I can write stuff."

They live in one of the many rectangle-shaped states in Flyover Country with their spouse, children, and pets.

This bio is much too strange to have been written by a chatbot, but if you need further verification that *Ancilla, Morsels: Tales of Love and Passion,* and *Excavations* were written by a living person, the author has an online presence.

AUTHOR'S ONLINE AUTHORIAL PRESENCE AS AN AUTHOR BEING AUTHOR-Y:

Goodreads – https://goodreads.com/author/show/47646299.Sera_Maddox_Drake

Reedsy – https://reedsy.com/discovery/user/seradrakeauthor

Wattpad – https://wattpad.com/user/SeraDrake

Medium blog – https://medium.com/@seramaddoxdrake

SOCIAL MEDIA TO FUTHER DEMONSTRATE THAT THE AUTHOR IS NOR A FRAKKING TOASTER:

Bluesky – https://bsky.app/profile/seramaddoxdrake.bsky.social

Facebook – https://facebook.com/sera.maddox.drake

Instagram – https://instagram.com/seradrakethebookwyrm

Pinterest – https://pinterest.com/SeraDraketheBookwyrm

YouTube – https://www.youtube.com/@SerafinDrake

But don't look on TikTok. The author has a severe nano allergy to pixels and avoids TikTok to avoid triggering theirself.

Nobody is thirstier than a self-published author. If you liked this book, please leave a review somewhere.

SECOND EDITION
ILLUSTRATED BY THE
AUTHOR

ANCILLA

MASTER, TEACH ME

...gic and philosophy sandwiched
...between some of the hottest
...nes I've read in recent years...
... it" – Hannah Gonzalez,
...Discovery ★★★★

"If stealing romances are your jam, this is the book for you.
Additionally, readers of literary fiction who love stimulating
stories with philosophical and emotional themes at play will
also find plenty to love about this novel. Sera Maddox Drake's
storytelling style is refreshingly unique and authentic." –
Pikasho Deka, Reader's Favorite ★★★★★

HUMAN
AUTHORED
At Authors Guild

SERA MADDOX DRAKE

Things an autistic, bisexual bookworm can find in a library: Books.
Periodicals. Kinky vampire librarians... Wait. Stop. Kinky vampire librarians?
Yes. And magic. And the most profound love she has ever known.

"Each story is only a tiny snapshot, and left me wanting more... Drake is a pro at playing with the reader's emotions in a way that I am slightly terrified of" - Hannah Gonzalez, Reedsy Discovery ★★★★★

HUMAN AUTHORED
Authors Guild

MORSELS

TALES OF LOVE AND PASSION

SERA MADDOX DRAKE

"I'm a fan of Sera Maddox Drake and this collection of short stories really showcases their writing talent." R.A. Volt, author of *The Whore, Hard Ride,* and *Her Servant*

Need a quick bite? Here are some short stories that might satisfy you. Some are sweet. Some are savory. But be forewarned... some of these amuse-bouches are as spicy as ghost peppers. They are marked accordingly.